D. Bowles

Picture Perfect

Senior Authors

Roger C. Farr

Dorothy S. Strickland

Authors

Richard F. Abrahamson ♦ Alma Flor Ada ♦ Barbara Bowen Coulter

Bernice E. Cullinan ♦ Margaret A. Gallego

W. Dorsey Hammond

Nancy Roser ♦ Junko Yokota ♦ Hallie Kay Yopp

Senior Consultant

Asa G. Hilliard III

Consultants

V. Kanani Choy ♦ Lee Bennett Hopkins ♦ Stephen Krashen ♦ Rosalia Salinas

Harcourt Brace & Company

Orlando Atlanta Austin Boston San Francisco Chicago Dallas New York Toronto London

Copyright © 1997 by Harcourt Brace & Company

All rights reserved. No part of this publication may be reproduced or transmitted in any form or by any means, electronic or mechanical, including photocopy, recording, or any information storage and retrieval system, without permission in writing from the publisher.

Requests for permission to make copies of any part of the work should be mailed to: Permissions Department, Harcourt Brace & Company, 6277 Sea Harbor Drive, Orlando, Florida 32887-6777.

HARCOURT BRACE and Quill Design is a registered trademark of Harcourt Brace & Company.

Acknowledgments appear in the back of this work.

Printed in the United States of America

ISBN 0-15-307806-5

6 7 8 9 10   048   99 98

Dear Reader,

   Picture all kinds of friends. Picture many
faraway places. There's a big world full of many
new people and animals for you to meet. Hurry!
Turn the pages of **Picture Perfect**. Say hello
to friends who laugh, cry, dance, and sing just
like you.

Sincerely,

The Authors

The Authors

What Can I Discover?

CONTENTS

Clap Your Hands

Lorinda Bryan Cauley

Clap your hands,
stomp your feet.

Shake your arms,
then take a seat.

Rub your tummy,
pat your head.

Find something yellow,
find something red.

Reach for the sky,
wiggle your toes.

Stick out your tongue
and touch your nose.

Roar like a lion,
growl like a bear.

Give me a kiss . . .
Do you dare?

Wiggle your fingers,
slap your knee.

I'll tickle you
if you tickle me!

Find something big,
find something small.

Spin in a circle . . .
but try not to fall!

Close your eyes
and count to four.

Now do a somersault
across the floor.

Spread your feet,
look upside down.

Make a silly face
and act like
a clown.

Hop like a bunny,
flap like a bird.

Quiet as a mouse, now . . .
Don't say a word!

Tell me your name.
How old are you?

Tell me a secret,
and I'll tell you one, too!

Purr like a kitten,
bark like a dog.

Crawl like a baby,
jump like a frog.

Count your fingers,
count your toes.

Wiggle your eyebrows,
wiggle your nose.

Show me a smile,
show me a frown.

Stand on one foot
and jump up and down.

Fly like an airplane
high in the sky.

It's time to go now,
so wave bye-bye . . .

Bye-bye!

THE ITSY BITSY SPIDER

As told and illustrated by
Iza Trapani

The itsy bitsy spider
Climbed up the waterspout.

41

Down came the rain
And washed the spider out.

43

Out came the sun
And dried up all the rain,
And the itsy bitsy spider
Climbed up the spout again.

The itsy bitsy spider
Climbed up the kitchen wall.

Swoosh! went the fan
And made the spider fall.

Off went the fan.
No longer did it blow.
So the itsy bitsy spider
Back up the wall did go.

The itsy bitsy spider
Climbed up the yellow pail.

In came a mouse
And flicked her with his tail.

Down fell the spider.
The mouse ran out the door.
Then the itsy bitsy spider
Climbed up the pail once more.

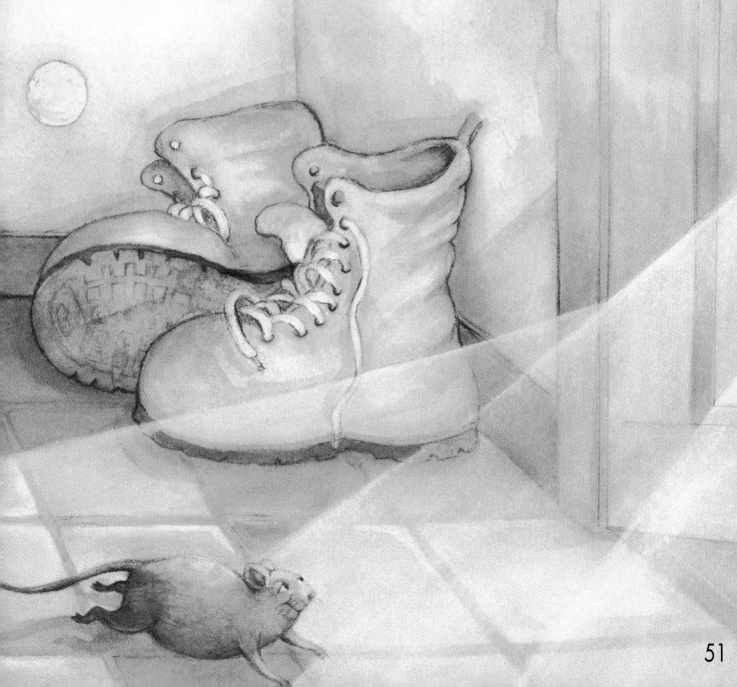

The itsy bitsy spider
Climbed up the rocking chair.

Up jumped a cat
And knocked her in the air.

Down plopped the cat
And when he was asleep,
The itsy bitsy spider
Back up the chair did creep.

The itsy bitsy spider
Climbed up the maple tree.

She slipped on some dew
And landed next to me.

Out came the sun
And when the tree was dry,
The itsy bitsy spider
Gave it one more try.

The itsy bitsy spider
Climbed up without a stop.

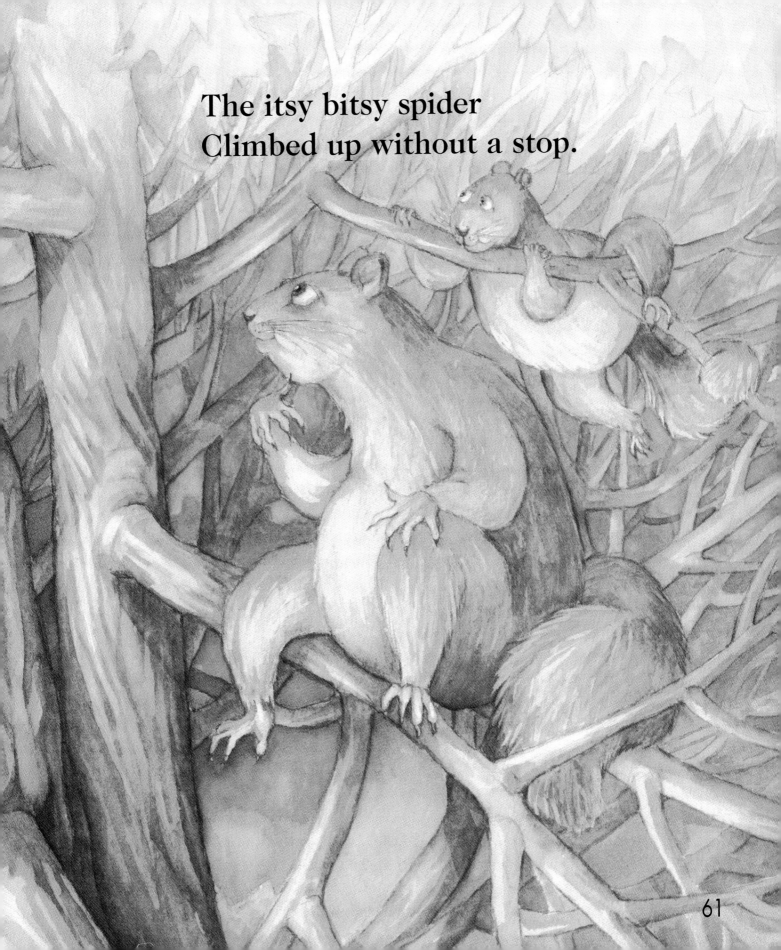

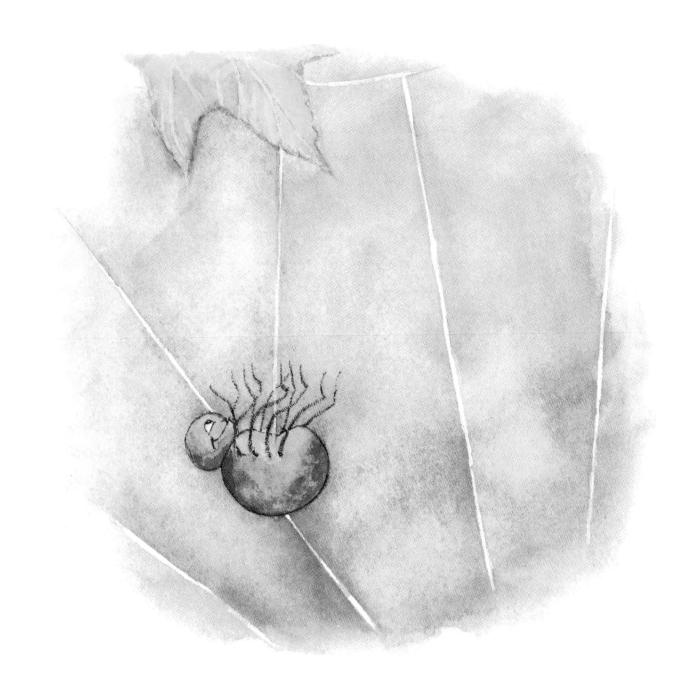

She spun a silky web
Right at the very top.

She wove and she spun
And when her web was done,

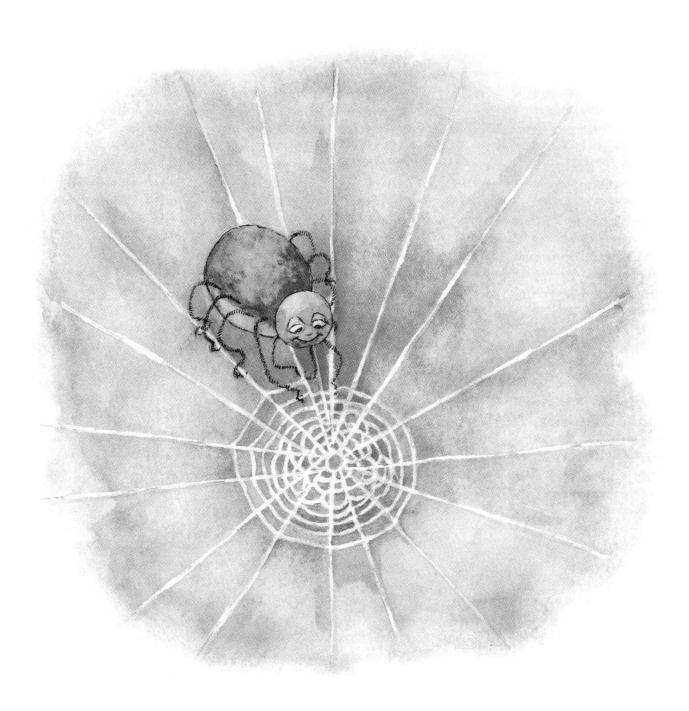

The itsy bitsy spider
Rested in the sun.

The it-sy bit-sy spi-der Climbed up the wa-ter-spout.

Down came the rain And washed the spi-der out.

Out came the sun And dried up all the rain, And the

it-sy bit-sy spi-der Climbed up the spout a-gain.

2. The itsy bitsy spider
   Climbed up the kitchen wall.
   Swoosh! went the fan
   And made the spider fall.
   Off went the fan.
   No longer did it blow.
   So the itsy bitsy spider
   Back up the wall did go.

3. The itsy bitsy spider
   Climbed up the yellow pail.
   In came a mouse
   And flicked her with his tail.
   Down fell the spider.
   The mouse ran out the door.
   Then the itsy bitsy spider
   Climbed up the pail once more.

4. The itsy bitsy spider
   Climbed up the rocking chair.
   Up jumped a cat
   And knocked her in the air.
   Down plopped the cat
   And when he was asleep,
   The itsy bitsy spider
   Back up the chair did creep.

5. The itsy bitsy spider
   Climbed up the maple tree.
   She slipped on some dew
   And landed next to me.
   Out came the sun
   And when the tree was dry,
   The itsy bitsy spider
   Gave it one more try.

6. The itsy bitsy spider
   Climbed up without a stop.
   She spun a silky web
   Right at the very top.
   She wove and she spun
   And when her web was done,
   The itsy bitsy spider
   Rested in the sun.

The Earth and I

FRANK ASCH

The Earth and I are friends.

Sometimes we go for long walks together.

I tell her what's on my mind.

She listens to every word.

Then I listen to her.

The Earth and I are friends.

We play together in my backyard.

I help her to grow.

She helps me to grow.

I sing for her.

She sings for me.

I dance for her.

She dances for me.

When she's sad,

I'm sad.

When she's happy,

I'm happy.

The Earth and I are friends.

Olmo and the Blue Butterfly

Alma Flor Ada
illustrated by Viví Escrivá

Olmo, sit up
and rub your eyes.

Look, a blue butterfly!
What a surprise!

Olmo, jump up.
Away you go!

Follow the butterfly high and low.

Hop on a scooter.
Away you go!

Follow the butterfly high and low.

Ride on a skateboard.
Away you go!

Follow the butterfly high and low.

Jump on a bike.
Away you go!

Follow the butterfly high and low.

Ride on a motorbike.
Away you go!

Follow the butterfly high and low.

Hop on a streetcar.
Away you go!

Follow the butterfly high and low.

Jump in a boat.
Away you go!

Follow the butterfly high and low.

Fly an airplane.
Away you go!

Follow the butterfly high and low.

Fly a chopper.
Away you go!

Follow the butterfly high and low.

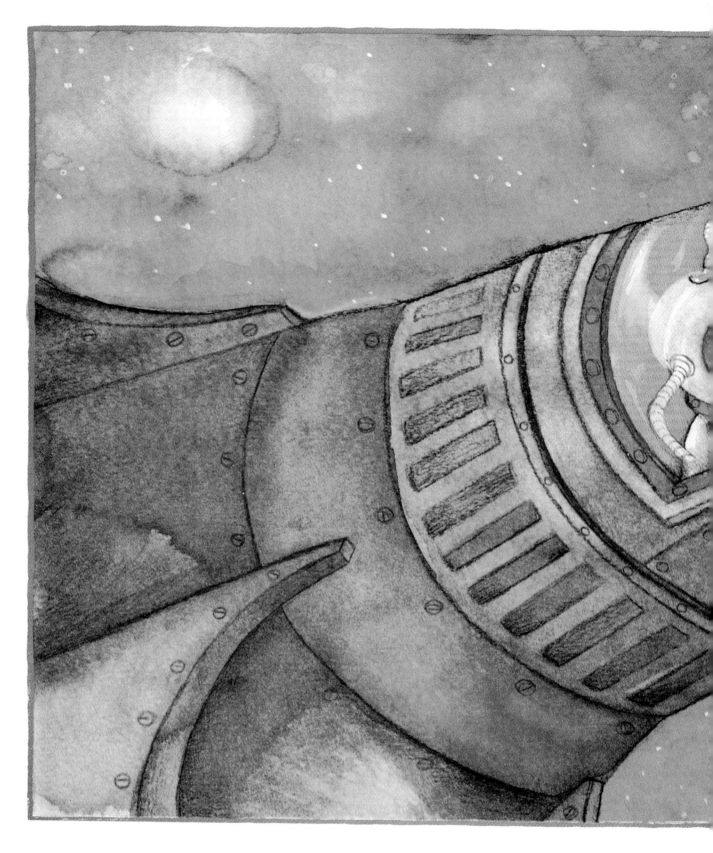

Ride in a rocket.
Away you go!

Follow the butterfly high and low.

It's always with you
wherever you go.

Follow the butterfly high and low.

Acknowledgments

For permission to reprint copyrighted material, grateful acknowledgment is made to the following sources:

Harcourt Brace & Company: The Earth and I by Frank Asch. Copyright © 1994 by Frank Asch.

Laredo Publishing Company, Inc.: Olmo and the Blue Butterfly by Alma Flor Ada, translated by Kathryn Corbett, illustrated by Viví Escrivá. Copyright © 1993 by Laredo Publishing Co., Inc.; translation copyright © 1997 by Harcourt Brace & Company. Originally published in Spanish under the title *Olmo y la mariposa azul.*

G. P. Putnam's Sons: Clap Your Hands by Lorinda Bryan Cauley. Copyright © 1992 by Lorinda Bryan Cauley.

Whispering Coyote Press: The Itsy Bitsy Spider by Iza Trapani. Copyright © 1993 by Iza Trapani.

Illustration Credits

Doug Bowles, cover art; Maryjane Begin, 4-5; Lorinda Bryan Cauley, 6-37; Iza Trapani, 38-67; Frank Asch, 68-99; Viví Escrivá, 100-127